The Whispering Heart

Vaidehi Batra

BOOK RIVERS
WE CREATE READERS

Published By: Book Rivers

Website: www.bookrivers.com

Email: publish@bookrivers.com

Mobile: +91-9695375469

1ST Edition: -2023

MRP: 299/-INR

ISBN: 978-93-5842-173-6

To my maker

Leena Batra.

I am because of you.

I hope you look at me and think

your sacrifices were worth it.

To Captain SP Singh

and

Dearest friends

without whom this would never be possible.

We are in this together.

[VII]

"I longed for love and sensed that in my memories."

CONTENTS

A Bittersweet Reflection

Yes! Nothing hurts me anymore.

For the bitterness, you brought into my life.

You existed because I wished for it

and prayed to the unfaced God.

My anger for you is greater,

But the love is sublime.

The feelings for you inside me

are still breathing,

but not alive anymore.

Soul-Bound

God created me,

befitting my soul,

As the undressed body.

My thoughts, though leashed,

kept screaming inside,

driving the heat of my soul

into my mortal frame.

Reminiscence

Cold hearts,
unpalatable memories,
low sounds,
melted bodies,
is what is reminiscent.

Elusive

The sun came recklessly,

Which I could not grasp in my own way.

It scorches but has no cure,

Because I know the blemishes will stay.

The sun came recklessly,

Life of Lies

Dear! If your heart feels heavy,

Why are you still carrying his latent love?

You hopelessly wasted your days

by carrying his dead love with you.

Wishing him to reciprocate your warmth

but in vain.

His insensitivity broke you from the inside,

And took your soul back to the void.

But dear, you are not willing to quit.

Whenever you look into his eyes

All doubts fade away,

And you decide to stay,

Living in his life of lies.

Despondent

After always being distressed and despaired,

She puts on one of those smiles

that weren't even real.

Letting the loops of hope get tinier

and craving for his love to blossom.

He would never sense the suffering.

Until he craves someone's love,

whose affections lie elsewhere.

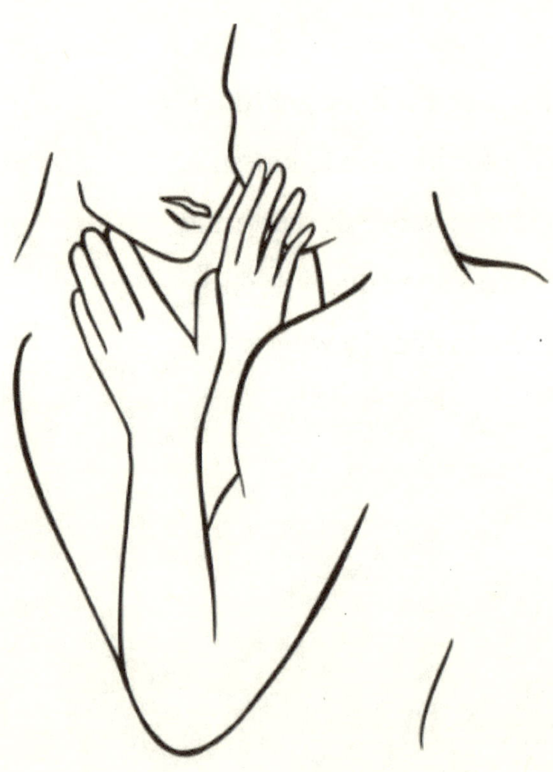

Unrequited Love

I loved you and still

I can't hold myself away from you.

You're constantly on my mind,

And the affection I feel is true.

But seeing you happy when I'm not with you

Leaves my soul wrecked inside.

The scars were never perceptible.

Words were always unsaid between us.

You held her hand over mine,

And I was the one who was crucified

with my Bible of Love.

Midnight Memories

Our first kiss in the night,

In the full moonlight.

With closed eyes

Holding each other skin tight.

Slow pecks around my neck

and the love bite you left,

the mark on my lips,

and your fragrance on my tips.

The way you looked into my eyes,

made my heart skip a beat twice.

Soul Searching

Be aware of dead souls.

Come across to make it yours.

Here and there, our senses are all lost.

The touch of glitter and the spark burst.

Black in colour, white in tear.

The Rainbow will bloom once you're here.

Deserving Patience

You know I deserve this.

But how could I wait more

To be fortuitous again.

[21]

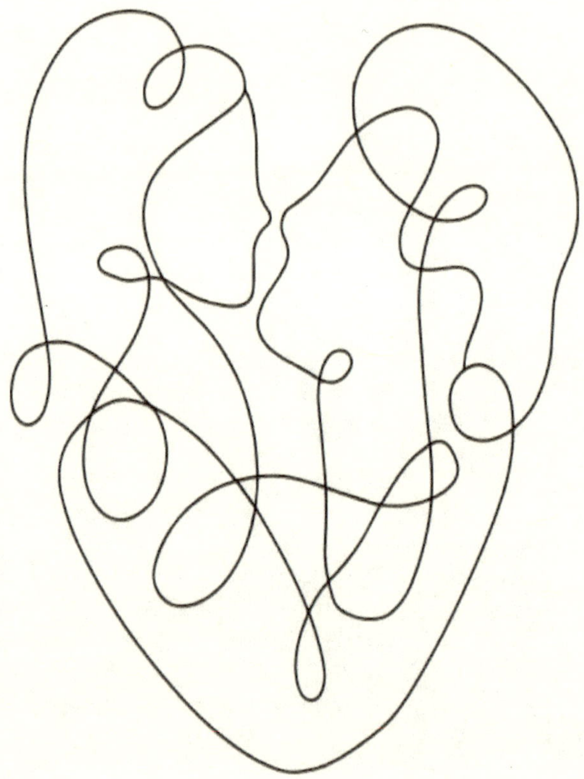

Soulful Love

Deep into my eyes,

All you would see

the diminishing love.

The soul inside me

Bore the burden of

your fading memories,

and I became the sunshine

with no mellowness.

Deep into my eyes,

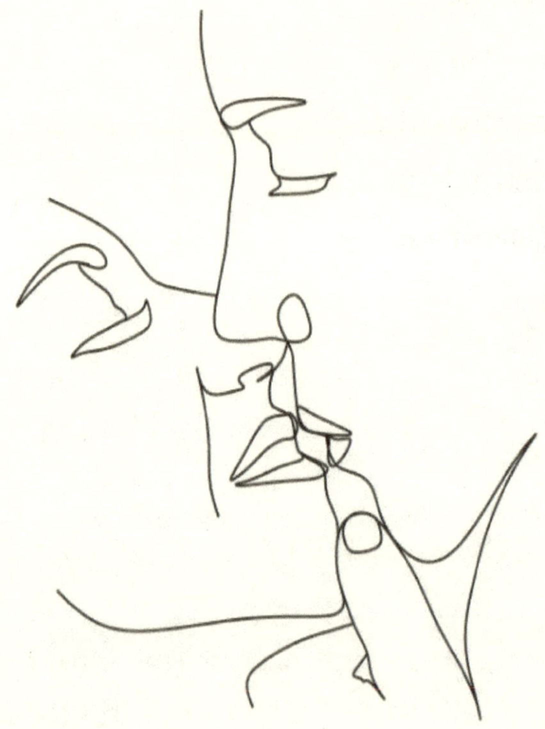

Ecstasy

You pushed me towards the wall,

When my lips touched yours.

My hands were lifted in the air and

Slowly floated towards your neck,

To feel the balminess of your body.

My eyes dimmed out

To feel the paradise on earth

When I caressed your soul.

Your fingers prickle me around my thighs

and my lips near your ears.

You were listening to the deep sounds of my wave.

Whenever I tried to look into your eyes,

You locked them with uncertainty.

A Heart's Interlude

I had a quiet interlude

Till my death for your return,

Decorated the dead roses you left.

Looked at the sky,

Just to see you above.

And always wonder,

Yours and mine,

Broken piece of the heart,

Were somehow alike.

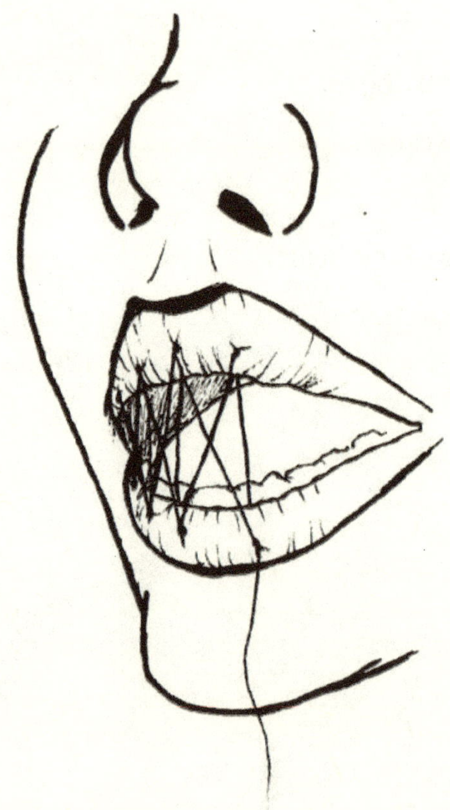

A Battle Within for Self-Acceptance

Just my words know the gist I engrave.

The expectations are making

the patch of my strength duskier.

My mind is raging inside,

and thoughts are seriatim out of it.

Lips are stitched,

and I have stopped believing even in myself.

What do I want?

What do I desire?

Inside me is a void with no hope of filling up.

I abominate myself when I act like the rest of the souls.

I'm feeling worn out from my retaliations.

Why do I constantly want someone to hold onto me?

It's overwhelming to be loved so much by someone.

Conflicted Love

The sip of love was not always what I wanted.

But when I got it,

It was all I wanted.

I became too much propensive,

Not to the person,

But to the love.

Authentic Love

Sometimes I just want to be close to your soul.

Want to forget all earthly myths,

And wish to feel virtuous adoration.

I wish someday you could feel the love

Inside my heart for you.

Imperfectly Perfect

I sometimes ask myself

Why someone will fall for me

Despite my many invisible scars.

Making intricate everything so often

and behaving childishly,

I know I am not perfect.

But always try to be exquisite.

[35]

Embracing Flaws

When I ask you to stay,

Will you hold my hand and stay forever?

We know the love is true,

But the sacrifices are immense.

When I expect you to hold onto me,

Will you do that forever?

We've got so many flaws,

and some can't be emended anyhow,

But when I look into your eyes,

All I can see is love.

And I just wanted to ask,

Can you stay forever?

Love is not enough.

But when I got you,

I wanted you to be one,

I know it wouldn't happen anyway.

But can we try to make it forever?

Watering Memories

I still water the dead roses you left.

Lost Love and Unfilled Expectations

You were so concerned about my desires,

But still, things went astray.

I drank the potion of love,

and malignancy went so deep into my veins.

I still adore your soul;

And dreaming of you is still necromantic.

But, like the ever-changing cycle of seasons,

Life has transited from the soothing warmth of summers

to the piercing chills of winters.

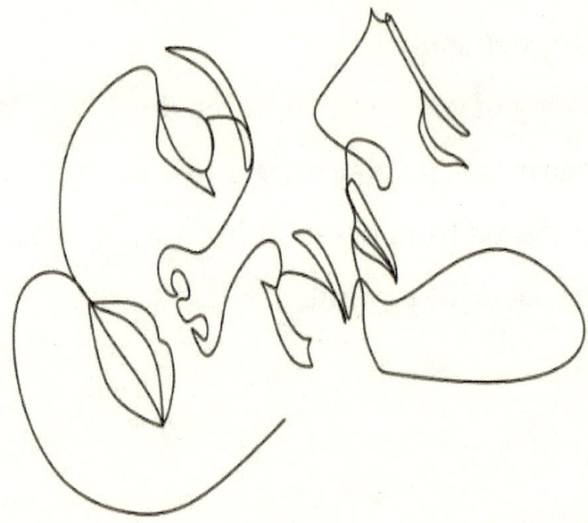

Love, Troubles, and Selfishness

Love and trouble are so similar.

Lips never ask for what the mind desires.

Hands never act as passing thoughts.

The heart is there only to spurt the blood,

not the feelings.

Only the tears in the eyes are existent.

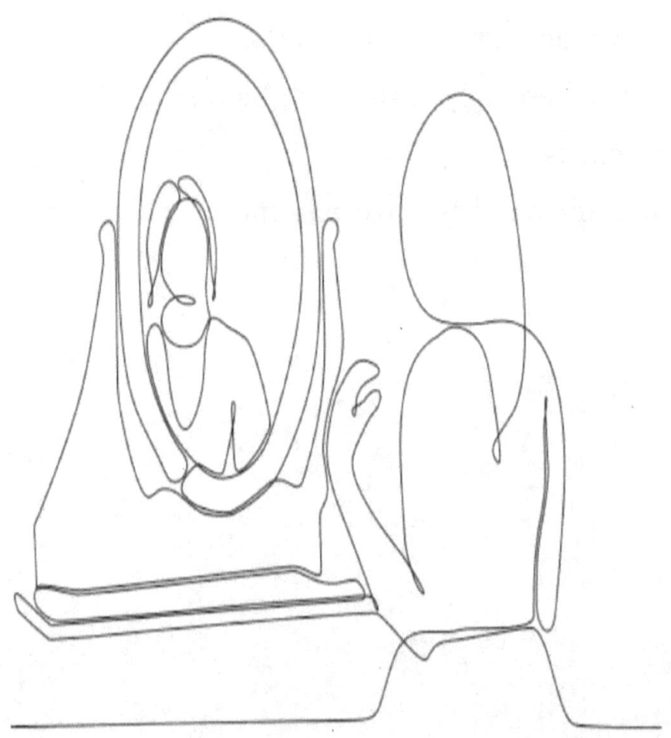

Finding Peace Within

I guess I have done a lot,

but today I need some self-time.

Life was a little harsh on me this time.

My breath is a little sluggish.

No words are on my lips.

No thoughts in my mind,

Just a little silence.

Time for my growth,

Time to revive errs

and time to sow new seeds in the garden.

And wait quietly to see them sprout.

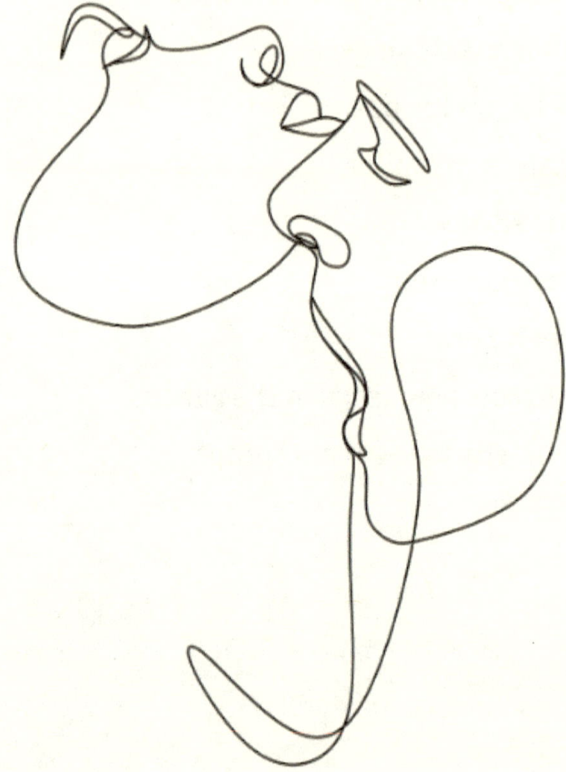

Time, Magic, and Love

I can see your inner scars bleeding,

but I'm too afraid.

What if I fail to help them in healing?

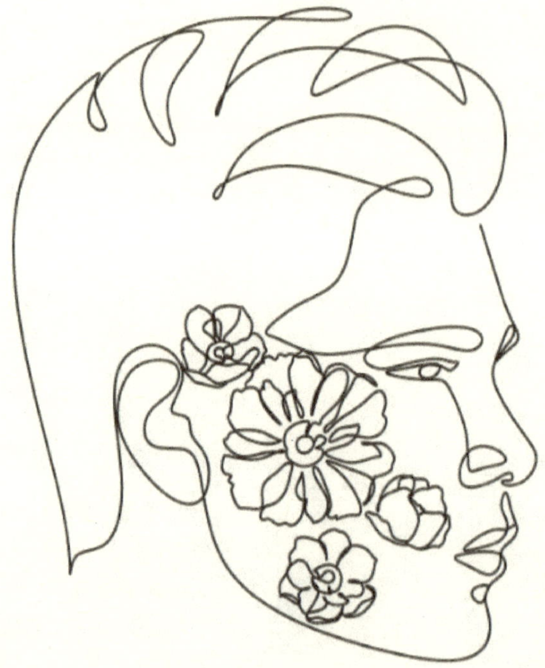

Sacrifice, Self-Love, and Growth

Many times,

You're the one who sacrifices,

and in the end,

You're the only one who is always willing to groove on.

Lowering your expectations may be a fiasco.

Sometimes you should halt and take a deep breath;

all you need is time to sprout and flourish.

You know you will revamp;

don't be harsh on yourself.

Things will happen when they are meant to be.

Unfulfilled Desires

I wanted it so badly,

The only reason it never worked.

Stargazing Amidst Darkness

Dark days never made her turned off;

she spent all those days looking up

at the dark shades of the sky.

The clouds were moving swiftly

along with the winds,

and the fragrance of flowers

was so overwhelming.

Counting the stars under the oak tree

and trying to hold onto them.

Tears might be cold today,

But not her memories.

Healing Wounds, Restoring Hearts

I desire,

One day, your wounds will be recovered

and you will love me the same as before.

Eternal Gaze

We don't know how long it's going to last,

so let me just hold you and look into your eyes forever.

Longing for One More Night

It's almost night,

and we cannot stay longer.

My eyes are asking you to stay

and hold me even tighter tonight.

But your hands are closing down soothingly.

But at the end of the night, I stepped aside

looking at you with dried eyes

departing away.

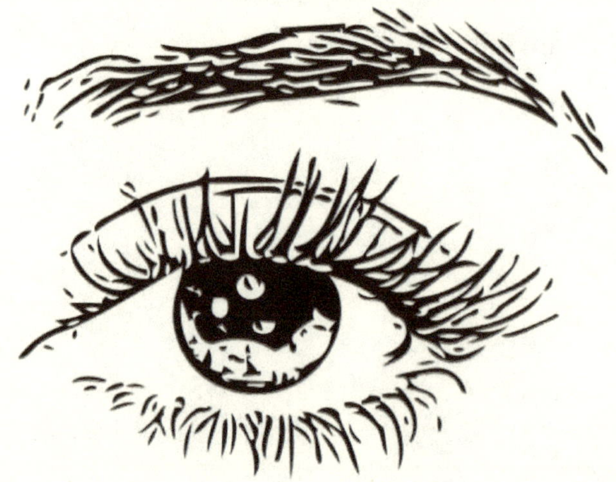

Words of Letting Go

And in the end

unspoken words became a smile

with tears in the eyes.

Cold but Dry

Are your hands warm?

Because mine are a little cold today,

A little dry and needs softness today.

You touched my fingers and slowly grabbed my hand,

A gentle kiss for all forgiveness.

The Devil in Me

What I did to you,

Was the devil in me.

And what happened to me,

Was my destiny.

What are we?

What are we?

Oh, stop and tell me.

Am I the only fool?

Or are you just trying to make me?

What are we?

Are clowns in the show?

Or romantic scenes in the movies?

What are we?

Having wine in the red dress,

Or maintaining distance cluelessly?

What are we?

-And it was all in the dreams.

The Romantic Evening Under the Stars

Wear the red dress,

I brought for you.

Let's go under the stars,

where I'll cook for you.

Looking at the moon and holding your hand,

Gently, then tightly.

You looked at me and said,

'The Moon Is So Beautiful, Isn't It?'.

But how could I tell you

you're not just the moon,

but the whole sky to me.

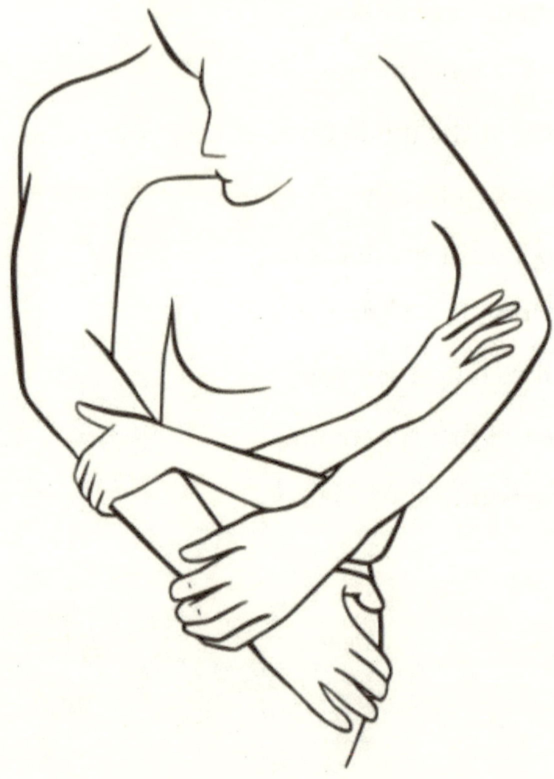

Yearning for Closeness

The desperation you can see

How close I want to be.

Aren't you too far?

Why don't you sit beside me?

Let me lean my head on your shoulder

While you sing a lullaby for me.

Don't let my hand go,

Let a little fondling on my fingers flow.

Sudden breath clashes,

Just a little closeness from being amorous.

Uncertainty in Love

Maybe you don't love me

Or you are totally in love with me.

Trapped in the Darkness

All the memories are flashing

in my dusky mind.

I pray to the darkness to carry away

all of my sorrows.

My body has petrified

and my mind has become desensitised.

My flesh feels hollow

and my veins are desiccated.

My eyes were drenched,

looking for the light

to carry me along

to where I belonged.

Journey to Neverland

Take me where you belong to.

Faultless

What happened to you,

is not my fault.

What happened to me,

is neither yours.

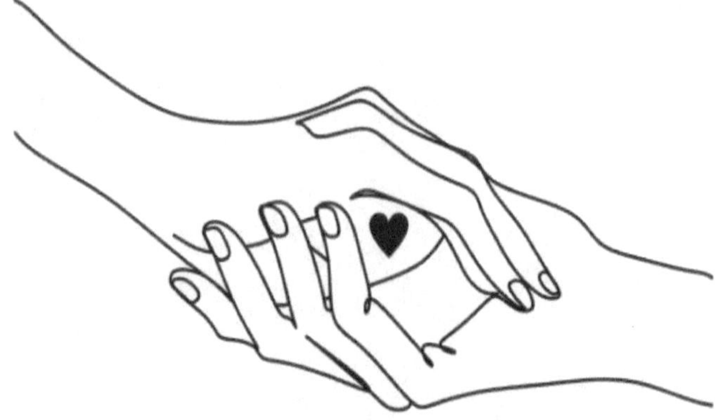

Blind Love, Opened Eyes

Love was blind between the two,

Blisters were on the heart.

Hard to lose that hand.

How could I love someone else?

Like you did.

The unopened letters you sent,

Have lost the fortitude to read them.

The love has been swapped.

All I see now is a new vista.

The Illusion of Love

You controlled me and named it as love.

[83]

Unveiling the Stars in Your Eyes

The stars I see in your eyes

Are they for me?

Why don't you show them to me?

Do they shine for me?

Or, like the sky,

There are many stars for the moon of me.

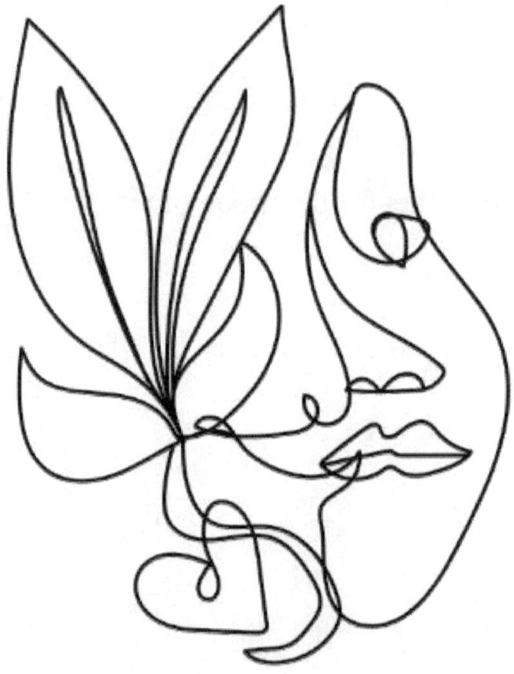

Moving On, But Forever You

Now my tears have dried off,

Now I don't scream your name in my mind.

Now memories don't fear me out,

Now your presence doesn't bother me anymore,

Now your voice doesn't make me want to look at you,

What is left now are only reminiscences.

The Day I Found My Soulmate

My mouth started twitching as I began to cry.

I tried to wipe my face with both of my hands,

but I was still sobbing my eyes out.

Unexpectedly, I felt a hand on my cheek,

gently wiping my tears.

I looked above,

and it was you.

Oh dear, how have I made you cry for me?

My eyes dried up just by looking at you.

All I could see was you,

Taking away all my pain.

I got up and wrapped you in my arms,

and a warm feeling spread through my heart.

-To The Soulmate

Nights of Dreamless Soul

Now it feels much safer

And nights are calmer.

By thinking that

You are far away now,

Intangible to my body and my soul.

Far away to give my heart

agony and despair anymore.

Now it feels much safer

The Allure of Fascination

The fascination can be perceived as

Dreaming of you with wide-open eyes.

Past love

That soothing intensive fragrance,

always came with me back home.

Your aroma in my clothes

to smell you again with each breath of mine.

I heard your voice in my head

calling me back.

Flashbacks I had when I touched myself again,

the way you touched me.

My heart started throbbing.

And my body started craving for you,

even more.

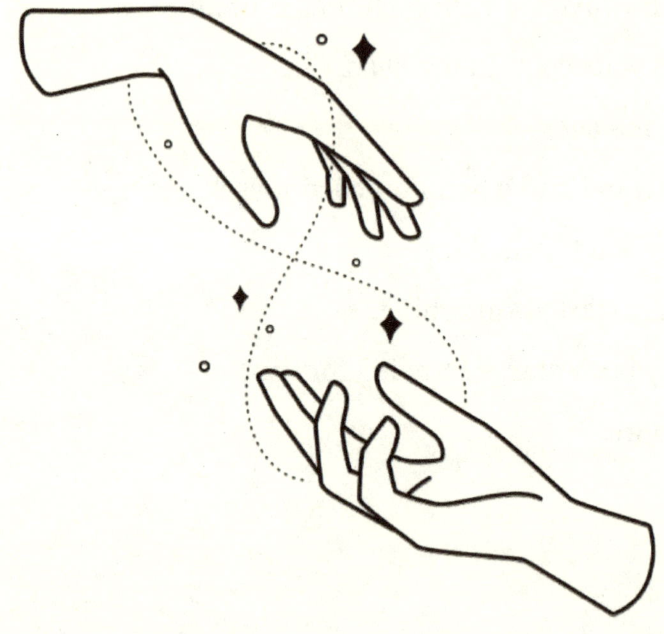

Healing Through Forgiveness

Still holding the threads of the relations

In my hands,

I left behind.

Just to introspect

how better it could be.

Words Only Hearts Talk With

You said it loudly

from the heart,

I heard it silently

Through my heart.

Bleeding Shadows

I heard the loud sounds coming from inside,

I wanted to escape but also wished to stay in that agony.

I have burned my heart in both ways.

Numb eyes and sober thoughts

Wondering in the clouds of souvenirs.

It bleeds from the inside,

And difficult to speak a word.

I always knew the end.

But I still give it all

To chase the blues away.

Midnight Longing

I couldn't sleep at night,

Pondering in thoughts of you.

Wished to hold you right away

and hear your breath near my ear.

Desire to run my fingers through your hair.

Slow-going kisses on your cheeks.

Tried to hold your hand

On those chilled nights,

When my body was cold.

Heard the birds chirping,

and I opened my eyes,

You were leaning towards my face,

and clasping me in your arms.

Envious Glimpse

I caught sight of you

Sharing the ripples of laughter with her.

Grooving on the tunes we had flickered.

I was envious to reveal,

My heart was sobbing

Seeing you writing amatory poems to her.

The Autumn would be the longest this year.

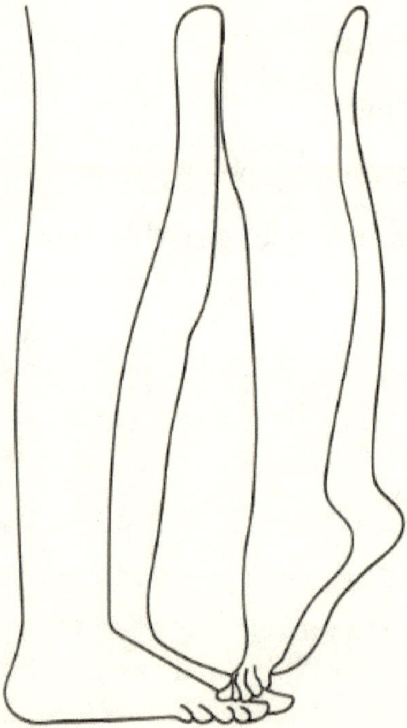

The Enigmatic Connection

How can I feel you?

When you are there.

How can I miss you?

When you are here.

[107]

Lost in Time

Whenever I close my eyes,

envisioning in my senses,

What your answers would be,

To every uncertainty of mine?

The hand, which were so cold,

Would you, this time, also love to hold?

I want to believe every word you say,

Which makes it harder to stay.

But I still want to strive,

For you,

For us.

Whispering Longings

You asked me to express myself.
And I started an inner monologue.
What if I say I still miss you?
Will you be honest with me?
I still try to memorise
the young days and nights we spent together.
You always tried to snuggle me around yourself,
Holding my hand tightly under the stars,
Those long, sleepy nights on your shoulder.
Can you still remember those days?
When you saw me in a white dress,
The way you gazed at me.
Your eyes were full of longing.
I felt the same when I looked at you.
I wished to hug you tighter,
When the eyes were in tears.
I could have asked you all of this,
But what would your answer be?
At this moment, you are still looking at me,
Holding back for me.
Miserable in my thoughts of you.
Can't you feel the warmth inside my eyes?
You asked me again, and
Here, I'm still cracked out.
But I decided to stay silent,
Put down inside the heart.

Drifting in Love of Ocean

Let me float on the waves of the ocean of your love.

Words Drenched in Tears

I don't want to feel what I write anymore.

I wrote things that made me feel saddest

at that point in my life.

Every word carries tears with it.

And the pages only know the pain I was in.

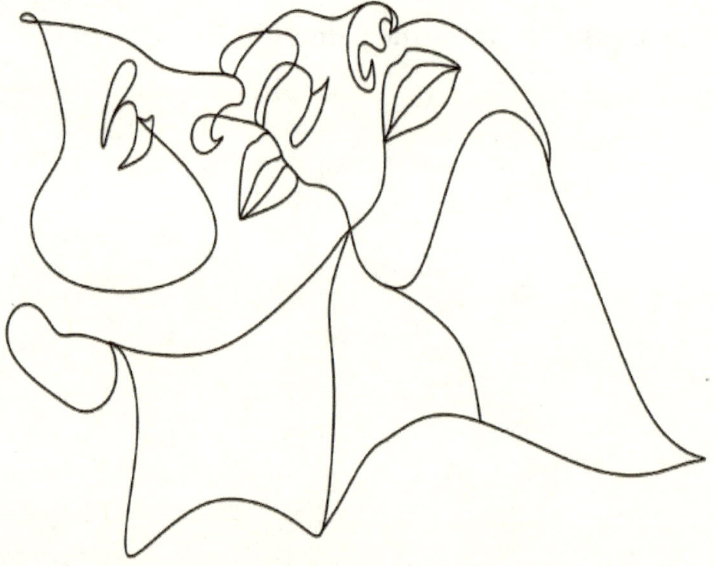

Echoes of Love

Most of the memories have faded away,

But still, whenever I gaze at you,

I realise that love will always be inmost

For you.

Sweet Remnants of Us

On my lonely nights,

The joyful moments of life,

The little things you used to do to me,

I miss everything about that.

I miss everything about you.

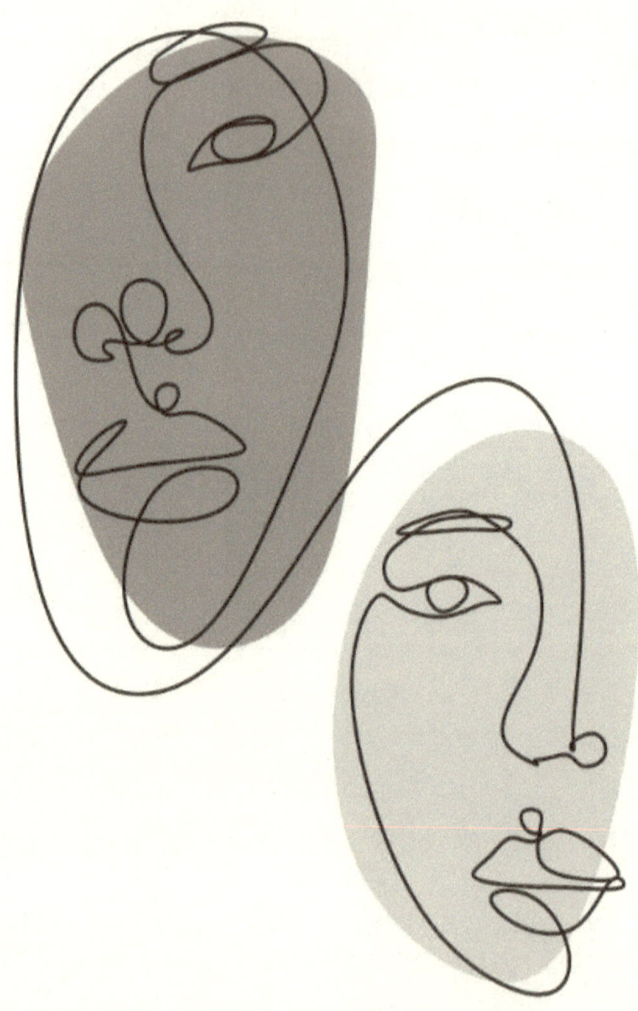

End with Heavy Heart

I do love you,

But I have to forget you.

For a future awaiting you

And for me.

I still care for you from my heart and beneath,

But this is the end.

Neither heavenly,

Nor gratified,

But this is the end.

Love's Resurrection

I cannot pray to God for your return any more.

But I promise if you do,

You will have my love

for real, again.

Wilting in Shadows

Without you,

I'm a sunflower,

With no sunlight.

Bouquet of Deception

Such a fool I'm to unsee.

How dead the flowers are

Which you got for me.

Eternal Sacrifice of the Moon

How much pain it bears

To meet the sun

It spends its eternal nights.

Hides in the day.

Watch from far away,

The romance with clouds and birds.

Stars are the only friends.

Remains silent in the dark.

Illuminates to enlighten the world,

But still burns silently in the light of the sun.

Eternal Sacrifice of the Sun

I will die every day,

So that you can see the beauty of the earth.

Even on nights,

To make you shine

With my light

from far away.

I'm happy to see you with stars,

While clouds and birds are busy with themselves.

I could have taken away your solitude,

But the days for the eclipse are still so far away.

Vibrant Hue

I was a dull painting on a grey canvas,

You came across it

and infused it with vibrant colours.

The Elusive Language of Love

Not everyone knows how to exhibit love,

It's always how the other one perceives it.

Rekindling Radiance

I left you bleeding,

And broke your heart into many pieces.

But I desire,

Your wounds reconcile,

Your eyes hit on love again

And slowly but surely

Your face beams back.

Shattered Dreams

Hope I die in my consciousness,

As I lost my senses around you.

I heard and bore the repercussions of being with you.

The glimmer of hope will always be sparkling.

Embracing Memories in Silence

Let me hug you one last time

And allow me to hear your breath.

Do not let me go,

Let the memories rewind once more.

Here is the last goodbye,

But I will never say it to you.

Fragments of Love

I broke your heart.

But inside,

I always held you back.

Fragments of Love

I broke your heart.

Lost in the Waves

I will let you go in peace,

knowing that we were painted in different shades.

I tried to swim in your waves.

But you were going separate ways.

I hope you had reasons to hold me.

When I was tied to a rope,

and the other end was in your hand.

You severed it,

and I fell into the ocean again.

I tried to swim, knowing I was drowning.

You were standing silently on the sands

Watching me peg away.

I saw you turning around.

The moment you were gone.

I could not even scream.

But I could feel that my heart was heavy

and the beats were sinking.

And I let myself go in peace.

Whispers of Love

Here once more,

I stand all alone.

Touched by the air passing you.

Your heart beats frequently.

Making the love waves

for another soul.

The stirring of love,

In the depth of my memories

Gazing into your eyes,

Finding the replies.

Why do I always end up holding your hand?

I tried to distance myself.

But my love craves for you.

My arms need your presence,

And my lips covet to whisper in your ears,

I know my love is not enough,

But I'm still here to repress every tear in your eyes.

I'm here to collect every chunk of yours

and stitch them together.

I'm here to hear your heart out,

I'm here for you,

every time you urge.

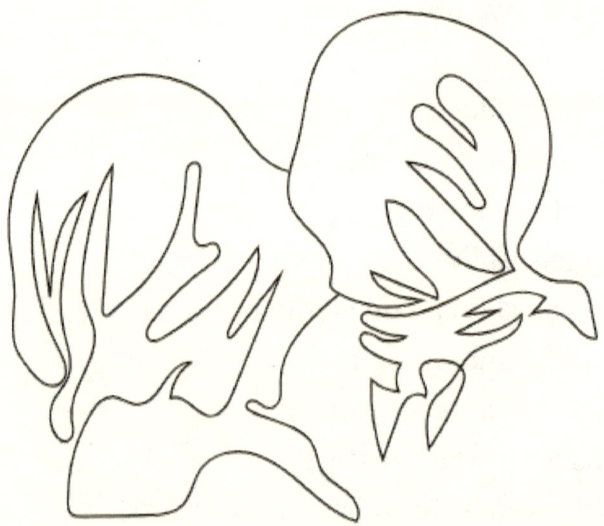

Dreaming in Your Touch

Missing each other like ages,

Craving for the touch,

You taught me how to be patient in love.

Sometimes the dullness of sundering over shadows my heart.

But my confusions overlap with the gleam I see in your eyes.

I want to live dreaming of you,

Feeling the strokes of your fingers on my face

And inundating me by telling

That you wish to be mine.

Where I clutch your hand

Whenever you need me,

And embrace you,

Whenever your arms ask for my presence.

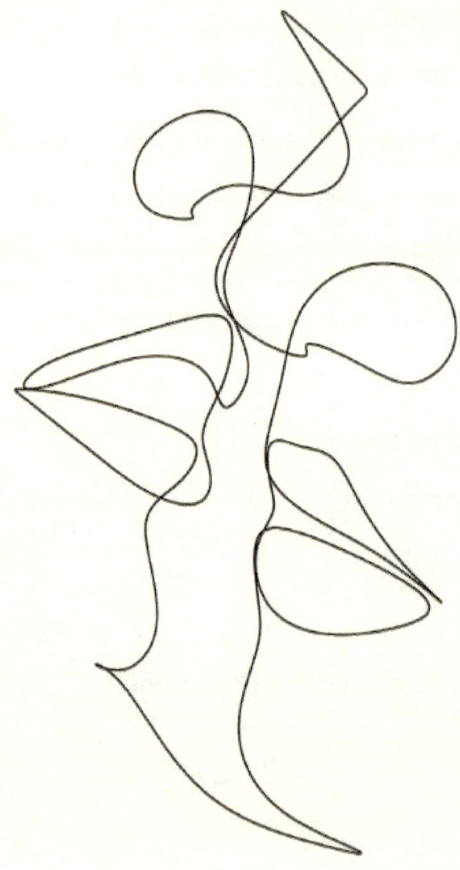

A Dance with Transient Joy

How could I ever let you go?

How would I mess with this air to recognise your absence?

I want to embrace you right now.

But should I allow you to look into these eyes?

I'm trying to hide these tears from you

And swing my face to let them flow.

The moments I'm holding inside me,

Shouldn't be caged by my emotions.

I turn towards you again,

realising how you're making this night

Magical enough for fairy tale stories.

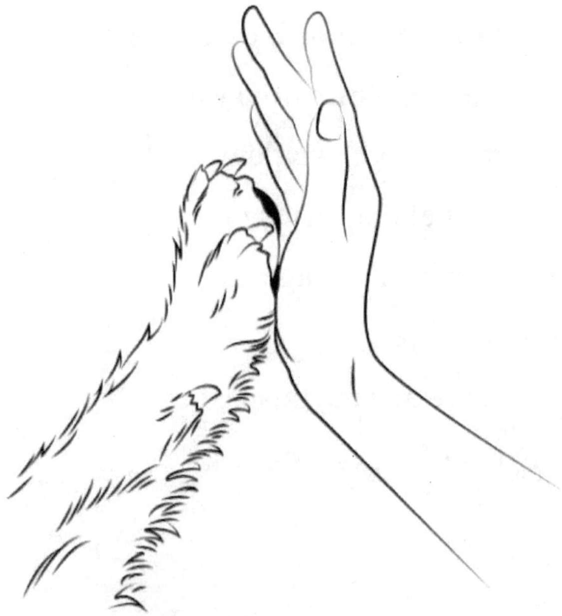

Unconventional Love

We aren't lovers,

But still, my heart beats for you.

We aren't friends,

But still, I'm by your side every time.

We aren't soulmates,

But still, I'm in tears seeing you in pain.

We are just us.

Diametrically opposed.

But still, our day never passes without a bear hug.

Colourful Resilience

And in the end,

She finally learnt

how to fill the colours in her life

With broken crayons.

11:11

It's time to make a wish.

And I desire,

By the replication of loving,

Bleeding, running and learning.

You will heal.

And love even harder,

To yourself.

About The Writer

Vaidehi Batra is an emerging author pursuing her studies in IT. She hails from a small town in Haryana, India, with a middle-class family background and aspires to search for her place in the world of fiction and non-fiction writing. Her strength is beautifully defining human emotions with a deep intensity and making a reader overwhelmed with thoughts of love, romance, and melancholy.

About The Book

The book is about the intense sentiments of a woman who is riding on a roller coaster of her relationship with her sceptical thoughts running through her wits and whispering in her heart with the hope of an answer someday.